Deadliest Diseases of All Time

E. coli

Randall
McPartland

Cavendish
Square
New York

Published in 2016 by Cavendish Square Publishing, LLC
243 5th Avenue, Suite 136, New York, NY 10016

Copyright © 2016 by Cavendish Square Publishing, LLC

First Edition

Website: cavendishsq.com

This publication represents the opinions and views of the author based on his or her personal
experience, knowledge, and research. The information in this book serves as a general guide only. The author
and publisher have used their best efforts in preparing this book and disclaim liability rising directly or indirectly
from the use and application of this book.

CPSIA Compliance Information: Batch #WS15CSQ

All websites were available and accurate when this book was sent to press.

Library of Congress Cataloging-in-Publication Data

McPartland, Randall.
E. coli / Randall McPartland.
pages cm. — (Deadliest diseases of all time)
Includes bibliographical references and index.
ISBN 978-1-50260-644-0 (hardcover) ISBN 978-1-50260-645-7 (ebook)
1. Escherichia coli infections—History—Juvenile literature. 2. Escherichia coli—Juvenile literature. I. Title.

QR201.E82M37 2015
616.9'26—dc23

2014049270

Editorial Director: David McNamara
Editor: Fletcher Doyle
Copy Editor: Cynthia Roby
Art Director: Jeffrey Talbot
Senior Designer: Amy Greenan
Senior Production Manager: Jennifer Ryder-Talbot
Production Editor: Renni Johnson
Photo Researcher: J8 Media

Printed in the United States of America

Contents

Introduction

What occurred in the Pacific Northwest in September of 2014 is rare, but it was no less a nightmare. Serena Faith Profitt, a four-year-old from Oregon, fell severely ill and died of kidney failure several days later. A playmate, five-year-old Bradley Sutton, was hospitalized and spent three and a half weeks on **dialysis**. He returned home but was placed on seven medications. Only 10 percent of his kidneys were functioning. The source of their illness: *Escherichia coli* O157:H7, commonly known as *E. coli*.

Three days after Serena died, three-year-old Brooklyn Hoksbergen died in Washington State. She suffered an unrelated *Escherichia coli* O157:H7 **infection** but died of the same cause: **hemolyic uremic syndrome (HUS)**, a kidney **disease** caused by the worst *E. coli* infections.

Even though public health officials know what killed the children, they don't know how the children became ill. Health officials found the **bacteria** in droppings of a goat on the Profitt family farm and suspect the animal as the source of the infection. However, another child in Oregon fell ill with an

Farm animals can be the source of a dangerous *E. coli* infection that can be passed on to humans.

E. coli infection. That three-year-old ate watermelon at the same place and time as Serena and Bradley, and some of that watermelon was later fed to the goat.

E. coli, as it's commonly called, is typically harmless. A **microorganism** found naturally in both human and animal **intestines**, it plays a vital role in digestion and helps the body absorb important vitamins from food. It also prevents the growth of dangerous bacterial species, acting much like a policeman for the intestines. There are hundreds of strains of *E. coli*. In day-to-day life, most of these strains are friendly. *E. coli* O157:H7, however, is not.

E. coli O157:H7 (the numbers and letters are used by scientists to describe the bacterium) is one of just a few *E. coli* strains capable of damaging the human body. First discovered in 1982 by scientists at the US **Centers for Disease Control and Prevention (CDC)**, it has since become a worldwide cause of severe diarrhea, and in many cases, long-term illness and death.

While *E. coli* can be deadly, there's no need for people to panic in fear of contracting it. The truth is, *E. coli* O157:H7 rarely kills and typically passes out of the body as quickly—if not as easily—as it enters. To protect yourself against *E. coli* O157:H7 or other dangerous strains, you need to understand where the bacterium is found and how it can find its way into the human digestive system. You should be aware of the signs of an infection, what you should do if you think

Drinking fluids and resting are the most effective ways to battle an *E. coli* infection.

someone has an *E. coli* infection, and what you can do to keep from becoming infected. This book provides a wealth of information on how you can protect yourself against this potentially deadly disease.

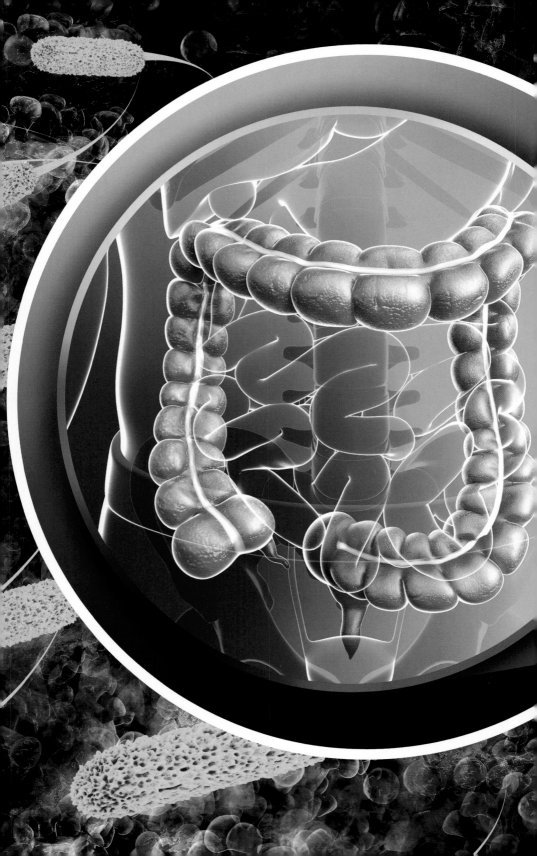

one From Good to Bad

S cientists have known about deadly strains of *E. coli* for just over thirty years. They did, however, learn of the existence of the bacteria almost one hundred years earlier. Theodor Escherich, from Germany, made the discovery of the microorganism and its role in the human body in 1885. Escherich was a bacteriologist, or a scientist who studies bacteria. He discovered the bacteria living in the human colon, a part of the digestive system. Escherich found that it could be blamed for digestive ailments such as diarrhea. The bacteria, known as *Escherichia coli* (*E. coli*), were named for Dr. Escherich in 1912.

Some forms of *E. Coli* are good for the human body. These forms can produce vitamin K2, and keep harmful bacteria from making a home in the intestines. However, bacteria can evolve and this is how *E. coli* O157:H7 started. To become a killer,

The *E. coli* O157:H7 bacteria can attach itself to the human intestine.

E. coli needed two things: it had to be able to make a toxin, or poisonous substance, and be able to attach itself to the walls of the intestines.

A bacteria phage is a virus that can infect bacteria. Scientists believe a phage infected a bacterium that could produce a Shiga toxin—the type of toxin found in deadly forms of *E. coli*—and also became able to make the toxin. It then infected *E. coli* and passed on the ability to make a Shiga-like toxin. This is called a Shiga toxin-producing *E. coli* or a STEC. This evolution happened in bacteria that can attach to human intestines.

Growing Problem

E. coli O157:H7 appeared first in the United States. The first two **outbreaks** took place in Oregon and Michigan in February and June of 1982. The victims experienced terrible pains and cramps in their abdominal region, or around the stomach. They had uncontrollable diarrhea often speckled with blood.

The doctors who treated them had never seen any such illness before. They ran tests for common diseases, but everything turned out negative. As they struggled to come to a conclusion, more and more people fell seriously ill.

Soon the CDC—a government agency that studies diseases and tries to prevent them—stepped in. CDC experts collected **stool samples** from the sick patients. They tested for salmonella, a form of food poisoning, and other bacteria that caused similar **symptoms**. Then they made an interesting discovery. They found that a large number of the samples they were testing contained a type of *E. coli* they had never seen before. They named this new strain *E. coli* O157:H7.

The scientists compared the stool samples of the affected patients with those of healthy people. They found that the healthy people's stools had no traces of *E. coli* O157:H7. This could mean only one thing: this strain of *E. coli* was not naturally found in the human body, and had somehow invaded the intestines of those being treated.

CDC experts also discovered that all of the victims had eaten hamburgers from the same chain of fast-food restaurants. The deaths of the two children in the Pacific Northwest in September 2014 were not considered an outbreak because there is no proven link between their illnesses. Therefore their cases are called sporadic, which means they are isolated. Finding the source of sporadic cases is difficult because the exposure to *E. coli* could have come from several places and scientists don't have enough clues to pinpoint a cause.

The scientists studying this first outbreak had many clues. They tested samples of frozen ground beef from the fast food restaurants and found that they, too, contained *E. coli* O157:H7. The sick people had eaten hamburger meat tainted with *E. coli*, which made a home in their bodies. The bacterium was

Hamburgers can be a source of food-borne illness if they are not cooked completely.

destroying their digestive system and was present in their stool. Somehow *E. coli* O157:H7 was causing these people—forty-seven in all—to become ill.

Second Helping

It was just a few months after this introduction to *E. coli* O157:H7 that health experts had their hands full

again. An outbreak occurred in Ontario, Canada, at a home for the elderly. In November of 1982, thirty-one of the 353 people at the home fell ill with painful stomach cramps and bloody diarrhea. **Epidemiologists** were called in to investigate.

Epidemiologists are people who study and track diseases in specific populations—such as the population of people at the home. They found that *E. coli* O157:H7 was present in more than half of the victims' stool. They traced the contamination to a meal that had just been served to the residents that included hamburgers. They also found that some of the victims wound up with *E. coli* without taking one bite of the **contaminated** meat.

The scientists determined that the bacteria had been spread from person to person. The only way this could have happened was if hygiene was not adequate. That is, if people were sick with *E. coli* and had diarrhea, and they failed to clean up sufficiently, it was possible for other people to make contact with the diarrhea and also become sick. Because the *E. coli* microorganism is so small, even the slightest trace of it on one person's hand could easily make its way into someone else's stomach.

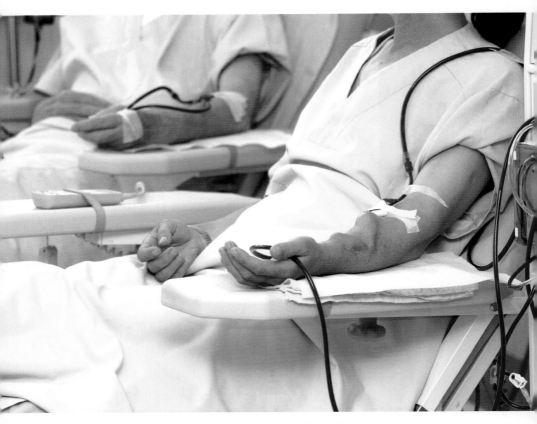

An *E. coli* infection can cause kidney failure, forcing people to undergo regular dialysis treatments.

In the Body

E. coli O157:H7 destroys the intestinal blood vessels. This causes the victim to bleed when they go to the bathroom. In more severe cases, the *E. coli* toxin then travels into the victim's bloodstream, spreading bacteria throughout the body.

Various blood vessels break apart. As the blood vessels break, blood clots form. Blood clots are blobs of sticky blood that clog passageways. This can cause strokes.

Often, *E. coli* damages the heart, the lungs, or the kidneys. Kidney problems—specifically a disorder known as hemolytic uremic syndrome, or HUS—most often lead to death in *E. coli* victims. If the kidneys stop working, the body can no longer excrete its waste products.

Almost one-third of those with HUS continue to suffer kidney and other problems many years after their initial infection by *E. coli*. For some, their kidneys fail to function altogether. This is known as renal failure. When renal failure occurs, a medical process called dialysis becomes necessary. Dialysis machines clean the waste from the victim's blood and help to bring the concentration of important body chemicals to normal levels. Other HUS victims experience medical conditions such as high blood pressure, seizures, blindness, and paralysis. However, less than 5 percent of those who develop HUS and receive medical care die.

A Closer History

1885 Theodor Escherich, a scientist in Germany, discovers a strange bacteria living in the human intestines. The bacteria are later named *E. coli*.

THEODOR ESCHERICH

German-Austrian pediatrician and professor Theodor Escherich discovered the bacterium *Escherichia coli*, which was named after him in 1919.

1972 The US Congress passes the Clean Water Act, requiring wastewater treatment plants to prevent polluted water from entering the drinking-water supply.

1975 The US Centers for Disease Control and Prevention (CDC) discovers *E. coli* O157:H7.

1982 Two outbreaks of intestinal illness take place in Oregon and Michigan in February and June; CDC scientists determine the cause is *E. coli* O157:H7.

1992–1993 A large outbreak takes place between November 1992 and February 1993 in Washington, Idaho, California, and Nevada; among the fifty-five people who fall ill, four die.

1994 Seventy people fall ill in an *E. coli* outbreak in Scotland due to contaminated milk.

1998 The Hazards Analysis and Critical Control Points Program requires meat processing plants to set up checkpoints to keep **pathogens** (microorganisms that can cause disease) from contaminating meat.

1999 The United States Department of Agriculture (USDA) approves irradiation for processing meat.

1999 An outbreak traced to water at the Washington County Fair in Upstate New York sickens one thousand people. Eight children are placed on dialysis; one child and one elderly man die.

2006 An estimated 199 cases of *E. coli* infection across twenty-six states are traced to spinach bagged in California. Three people die and about thirty-one develop a case of HUS.

2011 Outbreak of a new strain of deadly *E. coli* in Europe kills at least fifty people and infects more than four thousand.

2014 Clover sprouts are blamed for an outbreak that sicken seventeen people in five states. Among them, seven need to be hospitalized.

two A New Strain

A different new form of deadly *E. Coli*, 0104:H4, hit Europe hard in 2011. It infected more than four thousand people and killed fifty. One of the people who died was from the United States. The incident was the worst outbreak of a food-borne illness in history.

There are major differences between O104:H4 and the O157:H7 strain that started in the United States. One is that about one thousand of the four thousand people in Europe who became ill, or 25 percent, developed HUS. Dr. Robert Tauxe of the CDC said there never had been such a high rate of acute kidney failure in an outbreak. "That makes this an extraordinarily large and severe event," he said to the *New York Times*. About 5 to 10 percent of O157:H7 cases develop HUS.

The second big difference is that young and middle-aged adults suffered HUS at the same rate as

A German farmer plows under his crop during a 2011 outbreak.

children in the outbreak in Europe. Two-thirds of the victims were women. *E. coli* targeted mostly children and the elderly in the United States.

The third difference is that antibiotics seem to work on O414:H4. If antibiotics are given to those infected by O157:H7, the risk of HUS then triples.

The Shiga toxin found in the European *E. coli* was much stronger than the one that is most common in the United States. The O414:H4 virus forms mucus that shields and feeds it, allowing it to stay inside a person for a longer period. This helped make it worse. People infected by O157:H7 usually recover within seven days.

Researchers are not sure if the outbreak in Europe was a one-time event caused by perfect conditions or a sign of things to come.

Regular Outbreaks

Since those first few outbreaks of *E. coli*, the bacterium has turned up quite regularly throughout North America and the rest of the world. Most cases have been isolated—limited to just one or two unfortunate people who happened to eat contaminated food. Major outbreaks have occurred, and when they do the damage can be enormous.

The reason hamburgers make people ill is because ground beef is a major cause of *E. coli* infection. It combines meat from many different animals, thereby

Ground beef can pick up *E. coli* bacteria by coming into contact with tainted machinery.

increasing the risk of contamination. Cattle are a known source of *E. coli* that produces toxins. These toxins stay in the animals' intestines. When cattle are slaughtered and their meat is ground, it comes in contact with the contaminated intestines.

The *E. coli* can also remain on the machines that grind the beef. This way, the infection can be passed on to noninfectious cattle that are being processed. The infections can be passed on to chicken and pork that is placed on a cutting board that touched tainted ground beef.

Devastating Dinner

Stephanie Smith was a twenty-two-year-old dance instructor enjoying a Sunday cookout with her mother in the fall of 2007 when she ingested *E. coli*. Minnesota health officials traced her severe infection to a hamburger her mother had grilled.

Smith's illness took an awful path. First there were aches and cramps, then bloody diarrhea. Her kidneys stopped working and she suffered seizures that were so strong doctors had to put her in a medically induced coma for nine weeks. Afterward, she was paralyzed from her waist down. Smith can no longer walk or dance.

The source of Smith's illness was found almost by chance. Because she ate a mostly vegetarian diet, her mother thought the illness was caused by spinach blamed for another outbreak. However, Smith's aunt had several of the hamburgers left in her freezer. Health officials found *E. coli* in the meat that was a genetic match for a pathogen that had caused others in Minnesota to become ill. Animal parts used in those hamburgers came from many places, so the original source of the infection was never found.

Doctors at the Mayo clinic thought Smith's brain would never work again because of the seizures. However, she is living at her mother's home trying to relearn how to do some things. Her

E. coli

Stephanie Smith receives physical therapy after losing the ability to walk.

kidneys are still at risk of failure, and doctors don't think she will walk again.

In an interview with the *New York Times*, Smith said: "I ask myself every day, 'Why me?' and 'Why from a hamburger?'"

These dangerous forms of *E. coli* live in the intestines of the cattle and other animals such as chicken, deer, sheep, and pigs. The animals are carriers, thus these forms don't harm them. Humans do not produce these forms of *E. coli*; they must get them from another source. These bacteria reproduce quickly, doubling every thirty minutes. This is great for scientists studying the bacteria because they can grow a lot of it in a short amount of time. For others this is bad news because even a small about of bad *E. coli* can make them very sick in just a few days.

A large *E. coli* outbreak lasted from November of 1992 to February of 1993. Four states were involved: first Washington, then Idaho, California, and Nevada. Ultimately more than five hundred people came down with E. coli infections. Four people died.

Scientists investigating this huge outbreak determined that the spread of *E. coli* began at a single fast-food restaurant chain that served hamburgers. They traced the food back to its source and found that all the hamburger meat came from the same five slaughterhouses in the United States and Canada. Once at the restaurants, it was not cooked well enough before it was served. Health experts quickly issued a recall of all meat supplied by those five slaughterhouses and stopped the outbreak.

Not all *E. coli* outbreaks are caused by meat. The year after those five hundred people became ill from eating hamburgers, an outbreak took place in Scotland. This time cows were involved, but milk—not beef—was to blame. Most of the seventy people who became sick drank milk from the same local dairy. The milk had undergone pasteurization, a heating process designed to kill any dangerous microorganisms. No one had ever become sick with *E. coli* from drinking pasteurized milk. So what changed?

Part of the answer was found when the scientists discovered traces of *E. coli* in a pipe that carried milk from the pasteurization building to the bottling machine. They also found small amounts of *E. coli* on the bottling equipment and in a tank used to hold the milk. Finally, they found *E. coli* in some of the cow pastures, indicating that the ordeal had begun with the cows. The investigators never determined which of the sources was the root cause of the contamination.

More Nontraditional Sources of Outbreaks

Another *E. coli* outbreak happened in Massachusetts in 1991. This time apple juice had become contaminated. The apples most likely became contaminated when they fell to the ground and made contact with cow feces. When the apples were crushed, the *E. coli* spread from the surface of the apples and was mixed into the juice. More than twenty people were infected with *E. coli* after drinking it.

In 1999, well water was blamed for an outbreak in Upstate New York. A CDC spokesperson said that it was one of the worst outbreaks ever in the United States, as one thousand people became ill. There were 122 confirmed cases of O157:H7. According to the New York State Department of Health, sixty-five people were admitted to the hospital, and eleven children developed HUS. There were two deaths, a seventy-nine-year-old man and a three-year-old girl.

Tests were made on the well water and samples of O157:H7 matched those found in twenty-five patients. It is thought that heavy rains washed some of the infected cow manure into the well. The water from that well was used to make ice, lemonade, and snow cones.

The Most Unlikely Cause

Perhaps the most unlikely cause of an *E. coli* outbreak was the prepackaged Toll House cookie dough that infected seventy-two people over thirty states in 2009, according to the CDC. The states with the most victims were Colorado and Minnesota, each with six.

The people who became ill had eaten the dough before it was baked. The CDC sent out a reminder that prepackaged dough or even frozen pizzas should always be baked before being eaten. The flour in the dough carried the infection. The company that produced the dough, Nestlé, is now using heat-treated flour. The heat kills the bacteria. The company recalled 3.6 million packages of the dough.

Makers of cookie dough treat their flour to kill *E. coli* bacteria.

Most of those affected were under the age of nineteen and female. Thirty-four were hospitalized and ten developed HUS. One of the victims, Linda Rivera, who developed HUS, died after a four-year struggle.

Rivera had taken a few bites of the dough, according to her son, Richard Simpson. Her kidneys stopped working a week later and she went into septic shock. That occurs when a large infection leads to blood pressure dropping so low that it becomes life threatening.

Rivera had to have surgery to remove part of her infected colon and her gallbladder. Doctors believe the infection got into her brain, leaving Rivera unable to speak. What was unusual in Rivera's case was her age. Most of the *E. coli* victims are either elderly or very young. Rivera was fifty-seven when she became ill, and sixty-one when she died.

Dr. William Schaffner, a professor from Vanderbilt's school of medicine, said that it is rare for someone to struggle so long with an *E. coli* infection. He also said it wasn't the bacteria that killed Linda Rivera. "She never really recovered completely from her initial illness, and then developed a series of medical complications," Schaffner told ABC News.

One young person stricken by HUS during this outbreak, a four-year-old girl from South Carolina, was left partially paralyzed by a stroke.

Smaller Cases

Most cases of *E. coli* involve just a few people and receive very little press. After all, one or two people with stomachaches and diarrhea is hardly reason for newspapers to publish front-page reports. They'd rather focus on big news events, such as the major outbreaks where hundreds become ill. Still, when *E. coli* does make it into the human food chain, those affected certainly notice. Listed here are just a few of the *E. coli* outbreaks reported to the US Food and Drug Administration from years past.

West-central Wisconsin, June 8–12, 1998
Eight cases are confirmed by **laboratory** tests by the Division of Public Health, Wisconsin Department of Health and Family Services. Source of the *E. coli*: fresh cheese curds from a local dairy plant.

Tarrant County, Texas, June 9–11, 1999

Teenagers attending a summer cheerleading camp fall ill. Among other symptoms, they experience nausea, vomiting, have severe abdominal cramps, and suffer from diarrhea. A few of the cheerleaders have blood in their stools, which were analyzed by local authorities. Nothing is found. The stool samples are then sent to the Texas Department of Health and the Centers for Disease Control. *E. coli* O157:H7 is found in two of the samples.

British Columbia, California, and Washington, October 1996

An outbreak of *E. coli* O157:H7 is reported in Washington State on October 30, 1996. Washington State Department of Health officials determine the victims all drank a specific brand of unpasteurized apple juice. A total of forty-five cases were reported not only in Washington, but also in nearby California, Colorado, and in British Columbia, Canada. Most of those stricken with the *E. coli* were very young (the average age was five years old). One of the patients did not drink any apple juice at all, but happened to contract it through secondary transmission from another victim.

The juice company, once informed that it was responsible for the outbreak, voluntarily issued a recall of all its apple juice products, preventing further spread of the bacteria.

Lettuce is washed in California as a way to fight *E. coli*.

Rockford, Illinois, July 5, 1995

Five children are hospitalized with *E. coli* infections. Officials at the Winnebago County Health Center search for a common food source but cannot find one. Further investigation reveals that all of the children had gone swimming at the same state beach. The investigators decide to close the beach for fear that the children had contracted the *E. coli* by drinking contaminated lake water.

Seattle, Washington, November 16–December 21, 1994

A total of twenty cases of *E. coli* are confirmed through laboratory testing for the bacteria. Epidemiologists investigating the case determine the infections occurred when the victims ate contaminated dry-cured salami. Later, three more people fall ill in Northern California.

Spokane, Washington, July 11–14, 2002

At least thirty-four people attending a camp for cheerleaders at Eastern Washington University become ill after ingesting contaminated romaine lettuce. Experts believe the *E. coli* bacteria somehow made it from the farm to kitchen and then to the campers' plates when the lettuce was not washed thoroughly. By the time the outbreak is in full swing, at least one of the campers becomes so ill that her kidneys are affected and she is forced to go on dialysis. The outbreak isn't limited to campers. One of the victims is a person in Walla Walla who ate lettuce from the same produce company that supplied the camp.

Six States, July 2014

Raw clover sprouts are the cause of an outbreak that affects nineteen people in California, Idaho, Michigan, Montana, Utah, and Washington. Nine of those afflicted are hospitalized, but no one suffers from HUS. The sprouts were infected with the strain of Shiga toxin–producing *Escherichia coli* O121.

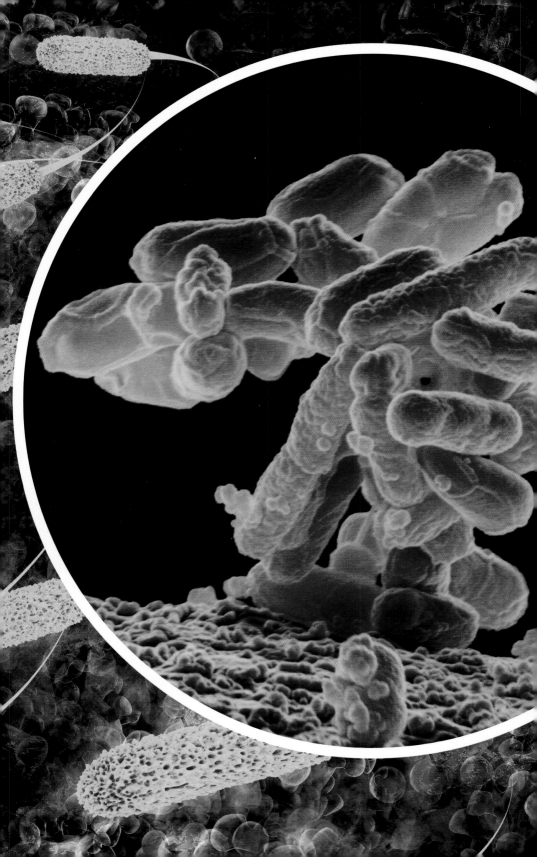

three An Ounce of Prevention

There is no cure for an *E. coli* infection. In fact, antibiotics can make the infection worse. Those who are ill are told to rest and drink fluids to prevent dehydration. Diarrhea is an unpleasant side effect of an *E. coli* infection, but doctors advise patients to not take medicine to treat it because it can slow the digestive system. A slow digestive system keeps the body from ridding itself of the toxins, which have to pass through the digestive system. The longer bacteria are in the human body, the more damage can be done.

People who do come down with an *E. coli* infection usually recover within five to ten days without any specific treatment. The elderly and the very young are at higher risk for developing life-threatening conditions because their **immune system**—the body's natural infection fighter—is often not as strong.

The *E. coli* bacterium is capable of reproducing rapidly, so a few can cause a bad illness.

Because diarrhea usually continues until the illness has passed, *E. coli* victims must be careful to avoid dehydration. Dehydration occurs when a person loses important body fluids. These fluids, specifically water, contain salts and sugars that are needed for the body to function. Diarrhea sends these fluids rushing out of the body. Severe dehydration is a potentially deadly condition.

The best way to avoid dehydration is by replacing the fluids and salts that are lost. For patients who have an appetite, this is fairly easy. Consuming plenty of soup, water, juices, and sports drinks can restore hydration. But sometimes people sick from *E. coli* are unable to eat and drink on their own. When this happens, they must be hospitalized and given fluids intravenously. Intravenous fluids are delivered directly into the bloodstream through tubes. The best way to fight the bacteria is to avoid ingesting it.

To understand why *E. coli* O157:H7 can be so dangerous, it helps to know how the bacteria can find its way into the human digestive system. Eating contaminated meats, vegetables, or fruits are a few of the most common ways, but other routes are also possible. *E. coli* is unique in that it only takes a few bacteria to cause illness. Most other bacteria must achieve large numbers before their effects become noticeable. This is one of the reasons *E. coli* is so dangerous—it doesn't take a lot to cause illness or outbreak.

Bacterial cells such as *E. coli* reproduce through a process called **binary fission**. In binary fission, a parent cell divides. When the process is over, there are two identical cells where before there was one.

Binary fission is an extremely efficient way of reproducing. The two bacteria resulting from the first split can each reproduce to make a total of four bacteria. Those four can do the same, making eight. The process can then continue repeatedly, resulting in billions if not trillions of offspring from just a single cell. Scientific studies have determined that *E. coli* can divide about every twenty minutes. In the human body, *E. coli* divides and replicates fast enough to create twenty billion new bacteria every day.

Waterborne outbreaks of *E. coli* are not common, but they do occur. Most tap water is perfectly safe to drink. Years ago, this was not the case. In 1972, the United States Congress passed a law called the Clean Water Act. The Clean Water Act requires cities to use wastewater treatment plants to prevent polluted water from making its way into homes. Today specific rules are designed to prevent bacteria such as *E. coli* from contaminating water sources. Strains of *E. coli* bacteria could potentially be present if the water contained fecal matter. The Environmental Protection Agency requires cities and towns to filter and disinfect water before it is distributed. Chlorine, which kills different types of bacteria, is usually added to drinking water.

Out of the Pool

Researchers at the CDC say that plastic and small, inflatable pools can spread what is called recreational water illnesses (RWI), which are caused by germs. Among them is *E. coli* O157:H7.

These pools are usually filled with water from a garden hose. The water can then be contaminated by children who have had an earlier illness that caused diarrhea. *E. coli* can remain in a child's system twice as long as it does in an adult's, up to two weeks, which

E. coli

Care must be taken to keep children's pools clean.

is why it harms them more often than their parents. Siblings who are bathed together are not in danger of infection if they swim together. However, if a child from another home swims in the pool, he or she can infect the siblings. This is why the CDC strongly suggests that day care centers not use these toys.

The CDC provides these tips for safely using these small pools.

- Do not enter the pool if you have been vomiting or had diarrhea.
- Take a bath or a shower and use soap before getting in the pool.
- Make sure any friends have not been sick before they get in the pool.
- If a child gets into the pool with a dirty diaper, get everybody out and clean it.
- Empty the pool after each usage. Clean the pool and leave it in the sun for at least four hours.

The drinking water on Mercer Island, Washington, was contaminated by an unknown source.

Still, *E. coli* can make its way into the water supply. This happened in late September of 2014 on Mercer Island, a suburb of Seattle, Washington. When bacteria were found in tap water, schools were forced to close and residents were told to boil, or purify, any water before drinking it. Restaurants had to throw out all foods washed in tap water.

Days later, a second test found a form of *E. coli* that showed the presence of sewage or animal waste in the water. Mercer Island gets it water from Seattle Public Utilities, which serves 1.5 million people. However, the contamination was restricted to a small area. The amount of chlorine pumped into the water was doubled and all traces of *E. coli* disappeared. However, the source of the contamination was never found. The tainted water did not make anyone sick.

Studies have shown that *E. coli* O157:H7 is able to survive in freshwater sources for several months. It often enters these sources through runoff from farmland that has been fertilized with sewage sludge. It can also seep into the water from septic tanks or leaky sewers. Once the *E. coli* is in surface water—such as streams, rivers, and lakes—it can make its way to shorelines along the coasts.

The waters of many popular beaches are regularly checked for *E. coli* and other **organisms**. If any contamination is detected, the public health authorities issue an alert.

Safe Eating

Most experts agree that O157:H7 is transmitted to humans primarily through consumption of contaminated foods, such as raw or undercooked ground meat products, raw milk, and contaminated raw vegetables and sprouts. The best protection against getting *E. coli* from your hamburger, for example, is to cook it thoroughly—until it is no longer red.

Because cows can carry *E. coli*, the bacteria can be spread through milk. Most milk is sterilized through pasteurization. Pasteurization destroys any dangerous bacteria. Raw milk, however, is not pasteurized.

If there is *E. coli* on the cow's udders or on the milking equipment, it is possible for the bacteria to infect the milk.

Another way *E. coli* is spread is through the consumption of unwashed fruits, vegetables, and other raw foods. If foods have been handled by someone with dirty hands or came in contact with contaminated meat, the *E. coli* can live on the foods' surface. If someone eats that food, they can become ill.

The **World Health Organization (WHO)** makes the following recommendations for handling and consuming foods.

- Make sure your food, particularly if it is made with ground beef, is thoroughly cooked and hot when served. The CDC recommends using a meat thermometer. All parts of a beef patty should reach at least 160 degrees Fahrenheit (71 degrees Celsius).

- Clean any surface used to prepare raw meat before using it again.

- Avoid raw milk and products made from raw milk.

- Wash hands thoroughly using soap, in particular after using the toilet, or after contact with farm animals.

- Wash fruits and vegetables carefully, particularly if they are eaten raw. If possible, vegetables and fruits should be peeled. However, it is

Thermometers can tell you when your meat is cooked properly.

not possible to wash all traces of *E. coli* from vegetables, thus bacteria can get into them. This is most common in sprouts, where seeds are often grown in countries with lower health standards than those in the United States. The bacteria can be in the seed and will be present in the sprouts no matter where they are grown.

- When the safety of drinking water is doubtful, boil it; or if this is not possible, disinfect it with a reliable, slow-release disinfectant agent. These are usually available at pharmacies.

- If a child becomes ill, make sure any toys, blankets, or clothing they touch gets cleaned thoroughly.

four Changing Landscape

T he battle against *E. coli* will likely never be won because harmful forms continue to evolve. However, scientists have learned a lot from studying previous outbreaks. They have become much better at tracking and controlling those activities. One example of this occurred in Colorado in October of 2013.

The Colorado Department of Public Health and Environment determined that on October 21, two cases of *E. coli* O157:H7 had matching DNA. The DNA was analyzed using a process called pulsed-field gel electrophoresis. This method, in simple terms, cuts the DNA from bacteria using enzymes and then views the samples from several angles using an electric field. This provides a DNA fingerprint. Scientists then send the fingerprint to other locations to see if there is a match anywhere else. This process likens to the FBI sending out a suspect's fingerprints to see if any other

Cucumbers were found to be the source of an *E. coli* outbreak in Colorado.

law enforcement agency has evidence that might help solve a case.

By October 22, there were four cases found in Colorado with matching DNA, indicating a cluster. There were no other places with *E. coli* cases with DNA that matched so scientists knew that Colorado was experiencing a unique exposure. By the next day the outbreak had been traced to a restaurant chain, which was notified. Bacteria were found in cucumbers grown in Mexico. It was the first time that *E. coli* was found in cucumber. The restaurant discarded the cucumbers, thereby preventing new exposures.

Medical scientists who study diseases are called epidemiologists. Epidemiologists are a lot like medical investigators. They learn everything they can about a disease—where it most commonly occurs, who it affects, how to control it, and, if they're lucky, how to destroy it. They do everything possible to stop diseases from spreading, and are often the first scientists on the scene when an outbreak occurs. In the United States, the epidemiologists on the leading edge of the fight against *E. coli* reside at the CDC in Atlanta, Georgia. These scientists study not only *E. coli*, but also other serious agents such as HIV (the virus that can lead to AIDS), other food-borne bacterium such as salmonella, and diseases such as cholera.

One of the main jobs of today's epidemiologist is to track the pathogen—a microorganism that is the

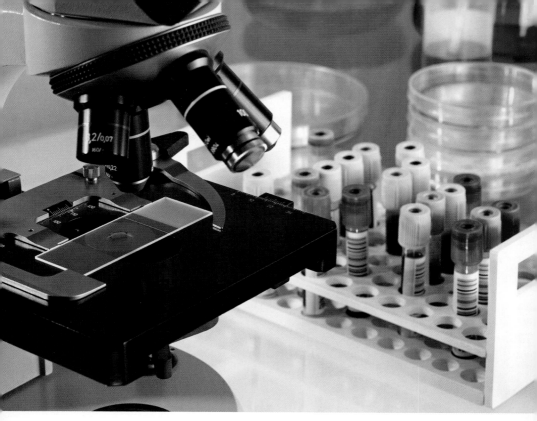

Epidemiologists collect blood samples when tracking a pathogen.

cause of disease—back to its source. In the case of *E. coli*, doing this efficiently can be difficult. Interviews must be conducted with victims, their families, and their doctors. Questions are asked about their food consumption. What did they drink? Do they remember exactly where they ate, what they ate, and the way the food was prepared, cooked, and served? The answers to these questions can supply helpful clues the epidemiologists can use to solve the case. By asking questions of all the victims, it is possible to find the source of the outbreak quickly.

Travel Tips

Not all forms of *E. coli* are fatal, but some that aren't are still unpleasant. One of the most common of these forms causes travelers' diarrhea—named so because it can ruin a vacation.

It is estimated that up to 50 percent of travelers experience diarrhea, depending upon their destination. The areas of high-risk are Latin America, Africa, the Middle East, and Asia. The areas of lowest risk are the

E. coli

When traveling, eat fruits you can peel yourself.

United States, Canada, Northern Europe, and Australia. Symptoms, in addition to diarrhea, are stomach cramps, nausea, and bloating. Bacteria cause about 80 percent of the cases of travelers' diarrhea, with most of those cases caused by enterotoxigenic *Escherichia coli* or ETEC.

Here are some tips for avoiding travelers' diarrhea.

- Drink bottled beverages, including water; avoid tap water and dairy products.

- Be sure that teas and coffees are made with boiled or bottled water.

- Make sure that drinks are not served with ice cubes made from tap water in at-risk areas.

- Brushing teeth should be done with bottled water.

- Beware of any contact with tap water in areas with unsafe water supplies. Avoid consuming fruits or vegetables that may have been washed in unsafe tap water.

- Try to eat vegetables and fruit (such as bananas and oranges) that you can peel yourself.

Another part of an epidemiologist's job is collecting and analyzing stool and blood samples from the victims. At the laboratory, the samples are analyzed for their chemical makeup, and examined under a microscope for telltale signs of the *E. coli* bacteria. If bacteria are found, then its DNA fingerprint is mapped.

Finally, once everything is tested and all the interviews are done, the investigators often turn to their computers for help. Powerful programs can analyze all the numbers and information and produce reasonable assumptions as to the cause of the outbreak and its source. Of course, computers cannot do it all, so these statistical analyses are used in addition to the work the investigators do by hand.

Once the outbreak is tracked to its source, the next step is containment. Health agencies will put out an alert to beef suppliers, for example, to let them know that a particular source of meat appears to be at the heart of the problem. The job of the epidemiologists at this point is to destroy the bacteria before it can claim more victims.

This is what happened in the outbreak in Germany, where lessons learned from halting O104:H4 outbreaks proved valuable. Millions of dollars of vegetables grown in Germany and Spain were destroyed. The practice ended when the outbreak was traced to sprouts grown in a region of Germany.

Each time an epidemiologist confronts an *E. coli* outbreak, or that of any other disease, they use what

E. coli

they learn along the way to reduce the risk that similar outbreaks will occur in the future. They study exactly how the bacteria made its way into the human food chain and then set up new barriers to prevent it from taking that same route. The goal is to make sure the same event does not happen again—especially in the same place.

One Among Many

E. coli is not the only organism worth avoiding when it comes to eating safely. There are many other common pathogens capable of making people sick. *E. coli* O157:H7 ranks fifth in the number of people it sends to the hospital. The first four are salmonella, norovirus, campylobacter, and toxoplasma. Forty-eight million people contract food-borne illnesses in the United States each year. Among them, three thousand die.

The CDC estimates that *E. coli* O157:H7 causes 36 percent of the 265,000 STEC infections that occur each year in the United States. It causes approximately twenty deaths per year.

five Uncertain Future for *E. coli*

Strides have been made in combatting *E. coli*, but a cure has not been found. One of scientists' primary focuses has been on not allowing the bacteria to get started.

One way to stop the disease is to change the diet of cattle before they are slaughtered. Studies show that cattle diets based on grain help *E. coli* in beef survive in the acid present in the human stomach. If those cattle are fed hay for the five days before slaughter, tests show that the number of *E. coli* resistant to acid is greatly reduced. Grain-based diets help the cattle grow, but that growth was not affected when the diet was changed for a short period at the end of the animals' life.

According to AmericanGrassFedBeef.com, animals who live all their lives feeding on grass in natural, open pastures carry significantly less *E. coli* than those raised in feeding pens. They are also exposed to fewer pathogens.

Food processors are working hard to keep *E. coli* out of the foods you eat.

Meat processors have spent millions of dollars trying to make their production centers free of *E. coli*. They have added large rooms in which they perform tasks such as scalding carcasses and washing them with acid. The agriculture department and the American Meat Institute continue to search for ways to make food processing better, but so far no one has been able to get rid of *E. coli* completely.

Scientists cannot estimate *E. coli*'s rate of growth or potential for future outbreaks. There's no telling when new strains of the bacteria will emerge, or if old strains will somehow mutate to become dangerous. There's always something else that can be discovered and something new to be learned.

Researchers at Washington State University have found that a naturally occurring essential oil made from cinnamon kills the top six non-O157 STEC in very low concentrations. One of the study's coauthors, Lina Sheng, said that the oil can be used on packaging for meat and vegetables or added to water used to wash meat, fruit, and vegetables.

Keeping *E. coli* out of produce is also a challenge. One effective way is to keep farm fields away from cow pastures. Cow manure can carry *E. coli* so it is important to keep it away from fields where crops are planted. The FDA recommends that produce exposed to flood waters caused by heavy rain should not be used for food.

Flooding can spread *E. coli* from cow pastures to vegetable farms.

Food Blasters

The Federal Government has approved a technique known as irradiation as a way to make food such as ground beef safer to eat. According to the electronic personal dosimeter website, packaged foods move on a conveyor belt under a radiation beam and does not touch radioactive materials. This kills food-borne pathogens, such as

E. coli

The symbol at left is required on packaging of all food products that have been been irradiated.

salmonella and *E. coli*. The Federal Government feels this is a safe way to handle meat.

One advantage irradiation has is that it is a cold process so food is not cooked. This means vegetables that undergo irradiation can be eaten raw. Hamburgers made with irradiated ground beef can be cooked rare, or remain pink inside. Supporters of irradiation say its use will decrease the use of pesticides. It is estimated that up to 25 percent of all food produced is lost after harvesting because of bacteria, spoilage, or insects. Irradiation also kills parasites and insects, but it does not kill viruses or *E. coli* living in the produce.

However, some people in the meat industry oppose it because it can change the color and taste of the meat. Tests have shown the presence of new chemicals and a loss of vitamins in meat that has undergone irradiation. Others are concerned that irradiation will alter the chemical composition of food. This process is also not allowed in food labeled organic by the United States Department of Agriculture.

One thing both sides agree on is that the best way to stop food-borne bacteria is for food processors to handle it properly so bacteria never becomes a problem.

In 2012, researchers at the La Jolla Institute for Allergy & Immunology found a molecule that has a role in fighting *E. coli* and other bacterial infections. Using this molecule, doctors at the institute are hoping to develop vaccines and treatments.

New Technology

Scientists are developing new technology that allows them to identify *E. coli* faster and easier. Researchers are now investigating ways to make *E. coli* bacteria isolation techniques more efficient. They are building special portable kits that can be used to detect *E. coli* in the field, directly in feces, in just a few hours. In the past it has been necessary to transport samples to a laboratory for further study. The results could take days.

Researchers in Kansas are developing genetic tests to find bacteria in cattle before they are harvested. This way they can stop the bacteria before they infect the food supply.

Doctors are also developing ways to make it easier to find *E. coli* that is actually in their patients. One such way is through testing a patient's saliva for signs of the bacteria.

The United States developed a database on laboratory testing of pathogens after an *E. coli* outbreak in 1993. It shares this information with health care officials. Public health organizations worldwide are continuing to work together in an effort to create an

Doctors constantly test for new forms of bacteria that can make you ill.

efficient international network that can identify and communicate information concerning outbreaks. Early detection of an outbreak can mean the difference between one or two people coming down with an *E. coli* infection and hundreds or thousands of people falling ill.

Shannon Manning, a molecular biologist at Michigan State University, told *Food Safety News* that her greatest worry is about the "ability of public health officials to predict the mutation of the next pathogen." Mutations are unpredictable. In those cases, she said, "scientists won't know what they are looking for and how to treat them."

Sharing as much information as quickly as possible is our best defense.

Glossary

bacteria Microorganisms that are sometimes capable of causing harm to the human body but are often beneficial.

binary fission Asexual reproduction by a body separating into two new bodies.

Centers for Disease Control and Prevention (CDC) An agency of the United States government that works to improve health and quality of life by preventing and controlling diseases, injuries, and disabilities.

contaminate To make impure or unclean.

dialysis A medical process used to clean waste products from the blood of people with nonfunctional or poorly functioning kidneys.

disease A change in the normal structure or function of any part of the body, characterized by specific unpleasant symptoms or signs.

epidemiologist A person who studies and tracks diseases in specific populations.

hemolytic uremic syndrome (HUS) A rare kidney disorder in which cells are destroyed and kidneys can stop working.

immune system The bodily system that protects the body from foreign substances.

infection The invasion of a host (a human being, for example) by a microorganism. Infections may eventually lead to disease.

intestine A body organ used to hold and excrete waste products.

laboratory A place used by scientists to conduct experiments and run scientific tests.

microorganism An organism that can only be seen with the aid of a microscope.

organism An individual living plant, animal, or microorganism.

outbreak A sudden rise in the occurrence of a disease in a particular area or population.

pathogen Something that causes disease, like certain bacteria.

stool sample A small collection of a person's feces used for laboratory analysis.

symptom Something that indicates the presence of a problem in the body.

World Health Organization (WHO) An agency of the United Nations whose purpose it is to promote physical, mental, and social well-being in people around the world.

Glossary

For More Information

Food Safety News

www.foodsafetynews.com

This website gathers news articles from around the world about the food we eat. It also contains a section on food-borne illness outbreaks.

KidsHealth

kidshealth.org/kid/stay_healthy/food/ecoli.html

Learn how to be safe in the kitchen, what foods to watch for, and ways you can help prevent contracting the disease.

Organizations

The Centers for Disease Control and Prevention (CDC)
1600 Clifton Road
Atlanta, GA 30333
(800) 311-3435
www.cdc.gov/pulsenet/pathogens/pfge.html

Interested in learning more about *E. coli*?
Check out these websites and organizations.

Environmental Protection Agency (EPA)
Ariel Rios Building
1200 Pennsylvania Avenue, NW
Washington, DC 20460-0003
(202) 260-2090
www.epa.gov

National Institute of Allergy and Infectious Diseases
NIAID Office of Communications and Public Liaison
31 Center Drive, Room 7A-50
Bethesda, MD 20892-2520
(301) 496-1884
www.niaid.nih.gov

The World Health Organization (WHO)
Regional Office for the Americas
Pan American Health Organization
525 Twenty-third Street, NW
Washington, DC 20037
(202) 974-3000
www.who.org

For Further Reading

Books

Benedict, Jeff. *Poisoned: The True Story of the Deadly E. Coli Outbreak That Changed the Way Americans Eat.* Brooklyn, NY: February Books, 2013.

Lew, Kristi. *Food Poisoning: E. Coli and the Food Supply.* New York: Rosen Publishing Group, 2011.

Marsh, Carole. *Hot Zones: Disease, Epidemics, Viruses and Bacteria.* Peach Tree City, GA: Gallopade International, 1999.

Parry, Sharon, and Stephen Palmer. *E-Coli: Environmental Health Issues of VTEC 0157.* London: Spon Press, 2002.

Ward, Brian R. *Epidemic.* New York: DK Publishing, 2000.

Index

Index

E. coli